► ESSENTIAL SURVIVAL STORIES

EXTREME COLD SURVIVAL STORIES

BY JILL C. WHEELER

Essential Library
An Imprint of Abdo Publishing
abdobooks.com

ABDOBOOKS.COM

Published by Abdo Publishing, a division of ABDO, PO Box 398166, Minneapolis, Minnesota 55439. Copyright © 2024 by Abdo Consulting Group, Inc. International copyrights reserved in all countries. No part of this book may be reproduced in any form without written permission from the publisher. Essential Library™ is a trademark and logo of Abdo Publishing.

Printed in the United States of America, North Mankato, Minnesota.
102023
012024

THIS BOOK CONTAINS RECYCLED MATERIALS

Cover Photo: Shutterstock Images
Interior Photos: Shutterstock Images, 1, 8–9, 19, 56, 62–63, 88, 99: Steven Chadwick/Alamy, 4–5; Roman Mikhailiuk/Shutterstock Images, 7; Tyler Olson/Shutterstock Images, 12; Wirestock Creators/Shutterstock Images, 16–17; Gary Hershorn/Corbis News/Getty Images, 22; Gopen Rai/AFP/Getty Images, 27; Anton Matushchak/Shutterstock Images, 28–29; Alaska State Troopers/AP Images, 30, 34; Library of Congress, 36, 48; DEA/Biblioteca Ambrosiana/De Agostini/Getty Images, 38; Print Collector/Hulton Archive/Getty Images, 41; Yvette Cardozo/Alamy, 45; Smith Archive/Alamy, 50; "The Adventure of Wrangel Island"/Vilhjalmur Stefansson/Internet Archive, 54; Kevin G. Smith/Design Pics Inc/Alamy, 59; Bettmann/Getty Images, 64, 67, 71; Cheryl Ramalho/Shutterstock Images, 74–75; Bain News Service/George Grantham Bain Collection/Library of Congress, 76; Frank Hurley/Library of Congress, 81; Library of Congress/Corbis Historical/VCG/Getty Images, 82; Red Line Editorial, 85; PA Images/Getty Images, 87; Sata Production/Shutterstock Images, 93; Sergey Nepsha/Shutterstock Images, 94; George Rinhart/Corbis Historical/Getty Images, 97

Editor: Marie Pearson
Series Designer: Maggie Villaume

Library of Congress Control Number: 2023939427

PUBLISHER'S CATALOGING-IN-PUBLICATION DATA

Names: Wheeler, Jill C., author.
Title: Extreme cold survival stories / by Jill C. Wheeler
Description: Minneapolis, Minnesota: Abdo Publishing, 2024 | Series: Essential survival stories | Includes online resources and index.
Identifiers: ISBN 9781098292201 (lib. bdg.) | ISBN 9798384910145 (ebook)
Subjects: LCSH: Survival--Juvenile literature. | Adventure and adventurers--Juvenile literature. | Arctic Regions--Juvenile literature. | Cold adaptation--Juvenile literature. | Wilderness survival--Juvenile literature. | Wilderness survival--Cold weather conditions--Juvenile literature.
Classification: DDC 613.69--dc23

CONTENTS

CHAPTER ONE
UP IN SMOKE 4

CHAPTER TWO
DANGERS OF EXTREME COLD 16

CHAPTER THREE
THREE WEEKS IN ALASKA 28

CHAPTER FOUR
ABANDONED IN THE ARCTIC 36

CHAPTER FIVE
HEROINE OF WRANGEL ISLAND 50

CHAPTER SIX
MIRACLE IN THE YUKON 62

CHAPTER SEVEN
AGAINST INCREDIBLE ODDS 74

CHAPTER EIGHT
SURVIVING EXTREME COLD 88

ESSENTIAL FACTS 100
GLOSSARY 102
ADDITIONAL RESOURCES 104
SOURCE NOTES 106
INDEX 110
ABOUT THE AUTHOR 112

The accounts in Chapters Three and Four mention thoughts of suicide.

CHAPTER 1

UP IN SMOKE

In mid-December 2019, 30-year-old homesteader Tyson Steele awoke in the middle of the night to a strange, steady drip from the roof of his remote Alaskan cabin. Fiery drips of plastic were coming into the hut, which was shaped like half a cylinder featuring a wood frame with a plastic covering.

Steele quickly pulled a pair of boots over his bare feet, and wearing nothing more than long underwear and a sweater, he went outside to see what was wrong. Standing in the −15-degree-Fahrenheit (−26°C) night, Steele was horrified to find the entire roof of his home on fire. With his closest neighbor 20 miles (32 km) away, help was unlikely to come.[1]

◀ Tyler Steele's hut was in the style of a Quonset hut. The shape of these huts makes them strong, and they are also easy to install.

There was little time to act. Steele rushed back inside, intent on finding his Labrador retriever, Phil. He stopped to grab blankets, coats, and a sleeping bag from his bed and called for the dog. He raced back out of the cabin, believing the dog was with him. He then went back in to grab his gun. Outside once again, he heard howling. At the realization that his dog was still in the burning cabin, Steele screamed in grief and collapsed next to the hut. There was nothing he could do to save Phil.

The fire quickly reached the area of the cabin where Steele stored his cooking oil, grease, ammunition, and a propane tank. Suddenly, explosions lit up the Alaska night. Steele spent the rest of the night and early morning trying futilely to stop the fire, throwing shovel after shovel of snow on the blaze. He focused his energy on trying to stop the fire burning around his food supply.

Around 11 o'clock the next morning, an exhausted and hungry Steele surveyed what was left of his home. The fire had taken nearly everything he owned. Now Steele realized that he would need to keep that fire going if he wanted to survive. He quickly went from trying to stop the fire to adding logs to it so he would not freeze to death. Surrounded by forest and water, he had nowhere else to go.

▲ Snow can be used to make an emergency shelter. If the snow is deep enough, a person can dig into it and make a snow cave.

In the meantime, he needed a place to sleep. He dug a trench in the snow just big enough to lie in and covered it with some scrap lumber and a tarp that he found on

⚠ Water poses a danger in very cold wilderness environments. If a person gets wet and cannot dry off and warm up quickly, they could die.

the property. He piled snow on top of the tarp for extra insulation to help trap his body heat. Then he crawled inside. Despite the cold, Steele was able to warm up enough to fall asleep. He slept off his exhaustion and began thinking about when—and if—he might be rescued. His clothes, including warm socks, were gone. His snowshoes, which would have

allowed him to venture out to seek help, had burned up in the fire as well.

TAKING INVENTORY

Steele had planned for emergencies as he set up his new home. He bought a special device that allowed him to use

KEEPING WARM WITH SNOW

Creating a cold weather shelter using snow can be an effective survival technique. Snow contains pockets of air and can block wind, two characteristics that allow it to work like insulation. Because heat rises, the warmest snow caves feature an entrance below the main chamber so heat from occupants or even from a candle can rise and stay contained within the structure. Survival experts caution that a good snow cave can take several hours and a lot of effort to make, and it ideally requires a large amount of snow, such as a four- or five-foot-tall (1.2–1.5 m) snowbank.[3]

satellites to communicate so he was never out of range, even if there was no cellular service. He promised friends and family that he would check in each week, yet he warned that he might be out of contact for up to ten days if he got busy.

On the night before the fire wiped out his cabin, Steele had just completed his regular group-text check-in with friends and family. The fire had started near where he kept his satellite-capable communication gear. As he surveyed the wreckage the following day, he realized no one would even think about checking on him for at least a week.

Steele knew he had no choice but to keep calm and draw upon the resources he still had. "I've dealt with fires before," he said. "A forest fire once, and a grease fire that almost burned down the lodge down in southeast Alaska, and I knew that I shouldn't panic, I should just be level."[2]

In the first days after the fire, Steele continued to see what supplies he might be able to salvage from the burned-down cabin as well as several outbuildings that had come with the property. Living far from the nearest neighbor and far off the sparse grid of Alaskan roads, the homesteader had stashed enough food for several years. However, the fire had melted his plastic containers and caused many of the metal ones to pop open. Grimly, he realized he had just 30 days of food if he rationed himself to two cans per day.[4]

In the outbuildings, he found an old, frozen snowsuit that he warmed up by the fire. He found gloves, some tools, and some old wool blankets. He found a piece of chalk, which he used to keep track of the days since the fire.

He also realized he needed a better shelter from the cold. After several days of sleeping in the snow shelter, he began work on a shelter incorporating the still-standing wood stove from the cabin. He used lumber scraps and other materials he found to build a makeshift tent around the stove.

> **My worst fear was making a mistake, and . . . slipping on something or falling through ice or getting to the point of no return with hypothermia or frostbite.[5]**
>
> —Tyson Steele, 2020

▲ In addition to the dangers of windchill on the human body, wind in snowy areas can whip up the snow, making it difficult or impossible to see far.

MAKING A PLAN

In the aftermath of the fire, Steele forced himself to work slowly and deliberately as he looked for supplies and constructed shelters. "I had no room for error," he said. "I couldn't rush, I [could] trip on something, break open my head. . . . I'd do about ten minutes of work and then just slow down."[6]

At the time, he had only about five hours of daylight per day. He knew he had at least ten days before anyone would look for him. "I realized it's now a mental game," he recalled. "I've gotta have some level of comfort. I've gotta try to be happy to get through this."[7]

DEATH BY EXPOSURE

Subzero temperatures, deadly windchills, and the ice and snow that often accompany them present an ongoing concern for people living in cold regions. These situations can lead to hypothermia, a condition that happens when the body's temperature drops below 95 degrees Fahrenheit (35°C).[8] Elizabeth Richards, associate professor at the Purdue University School of Nursing, said, "Untreated hypothermia causes most of our body systems to start to fail, eventually leading to failure of our heart and lungs, which causes death."[9]

In the United States alone, the National Institutes of Health estimates that more than 1,300 Americans die of cold exposure each year.

YOU GET USED TO IT

The human body has an ability to adjust to cold over time. It's why a cool temperature in fall can feel colder than the same temperature in spring, after the body has become more used to cold weather. Researchers credit this to the presence of brown fat. While the body initially shivers to stay warm, the body can also warm itself by burning brown fat. Research indicates the body creates more brown fat when exposed to cold temperatures over time.

SURVIVING UNDER ICE

In 1999, Swedish skier Anna Bågenholm lost control on the slopes and fell into a frozen stream. She was trapped under ice for 80 minutes. At the time of her rescue, she had no heartbeat and had a body temperature of 56.7 degrees Fahrenheit (13.7°C), the lowest ever recorded for an individual who did not die.[12] Because Bågenholm's body had cooled before her heart stopped, it required less oxygen. Doctors were able to slowly warm and revive her, and she went on to live with only minimal impacts from her near-death experience.

A global study of more than 74 million deaths across 13 nations also found that extreme cold kills more than 20 times as many people as extreme heat.[10]

Many people are unaware of how cold can be too cold. "It's safe to be outside if the temperature is 32°F [0°C] or above," said Dr. David Greuner of NYC Surgical Associates. "If the temperature falls between 13°F and 31°F [−11 and −0.6°C], you should take breaks from the cold approximately every 20 to 30 minutes. If windchill temperatures are 13°F [−11°C] and below, you should remain indoors."[11]

Greuner noted that windchill is an indicator of how quickly outdoor conditions can remove heat from exposed skin. The windchill index is a tool that accounts for the role wind plays in making the actual air temperature feel even colder than the temperature on the thermometer. Windchill represents the air temperature with no wind that would cause the body to lose heat as quickly as the actual temperature with wind. A temperature of 20 degrees Fahrenheit (−6.7°C) can be dangerous when combined with wind blowing 10 miles per hour (16 kmh). Moisture can also change the equation, as water transfers heat from the body at a rate of roughly 30 times that of air.[13] This is why swimming pools feel so good on hot days, but it also means people should stay as dry as possible in cold temperatures.

Cold temperatures can be deadly, but they are manageable with the right preparation, skills, and equipment. The stories of individuals who have survived subzero situations offer both warnings of behaviors to avoid and insights into how to stay alive. These stories also demonstrate that the unexpected can and does happen, placing people who do not normally deal with extreme cold into situations where their very survival is at stake.

Quick thinking and survival skills can mean the difference between staying alive and freezing to death. So too can preparation, creativity with available resources, and maintaining a positive attitude. By better understanding one's surroundings and the dangers they bring, anyone can increase the odds of turning a potential tragedy into an extreme cold survival story.

CHAPTER 2

DANGERS OF EXTREME COLD

Mention extreme cold and many people's thoughts turn to Earth's polar regions. Both the Arctic and the Antarctic are known for bitterly cold winters and short, frigid summers. Even in summer, the sun rises only slightly above the horizon in both regions. In the winter, the sun does not rise for months at a time.

These polar landscapes are dominated by glaciers and giant sheets of ice, which reflect what little sunlight the region receives and the heat that comes with it, preventing the icy landscape from melting. Even though they are covered in snow and ice, polar regions are considered deserts because they receive

◂ Some animals, such as penguins, are equipped to handle extreme cold. But humans need careful planning to remain warm in such an environment.

extremely little precipitation. The very cold air is unable to hold much water vapor, so there are few clouds and little rain or snow.

The northern polar region, the Arctic, is defined as the area above the Arctic Circle, which is located at 66.5 degrees north latitude. Most of the Arctic region is sea. The center of the Arctic, called the North Pole, is within the Arctic Ocean. It has an average winter temperature of −40 degrees Fahrenheit (−40°C) and an average summer temperature of 32 degrees Fahrenheit (0°C).[1]

On the opposite side of Earth, Antarctica is a continental landmass. The average winter temperature at the South Pole is −74 degrees Fahrenheit (−59°C). In the summer, the temperature rises to an average of −18 degrees Fahrenheit (−28°C).[2] Antarctica's extreme cold is an example of how the climates of Earth's landmasses are influenced by their size, their location, and the reflectivity of their surfaces.

While neither polar region receives significant solar radiation due to the low angle of the sunlight at the poles, the South Pole is located on land, and the North Pole is at sea. Large bodies of water, such as the water around the North Pole, do not experience as much change in temperature over the course of the year as a large body

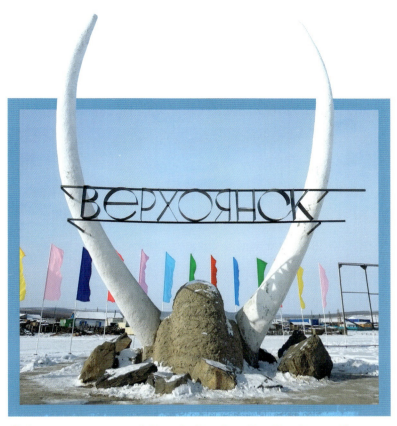

▲ A monument resembling the head and tusks of a woolly mammoth stands in Verkhoyansk to recognize the area as the coldest place in the Arctic.

of land does. Therefore, the water around the North Pole keeps that pole's temperature more moderate than the temperature around the land-based South Pole. For this same reason, the coldest place in the Arctic region is not at the North Pole in the center of the Arctic Ocean but rather in Verkhoyansk, Russia, which is located in the Siberian region of the large landmass of Europe and Asia.

Antarctica is not owned by any single country, and there are no permanent residents on the continent.

Meanwhile, only about four million people make their home in the Arctic region in Alaska, Greenland, and parts of Russia, Canada, Norway, Sweden, Finland, and Iceland.[3] More people live in the tundra and coastal regions located just south of the Arctic region.

Unlike the polar ice caps, tundra environments are not covered by ice all year. While most of the ground remains frozen in permafrost, the topmost layer of soil does warm up enough to support some seasonal, low-growing vegetation, such as shrubs and grasses. In addition to this small population, tundra areas also are home to animals such as polar bears, Arctic foxes, caribou, and musk oxen.

POLAR PLUNGE

Most Arctic residents are aware of the dangers of extreme cold, and most Arctic homes are designed to withstand the unique

HOMELESSNESS IN COLD CLIMATES

Some individuals experiencing homelessness camp outside year-round, even in cold climates. In Anchorage, Alaska, agencies serving unhoused individuals estimate between 8,000 and 10,000 people in the city spend at least part of the year with no permanent home. While many use local shelters, some individuals say they would rather deal with the cold than deal with the rules, noise, and curfews that come with emergency shelters. "It's a learned art," said one person about living outside through a frigid Alaska winter. "After a while, you just start getting used to it."[4]

challenges of the region. Extreme cold becomes more of a threat when things do not go as planned. There may be an unexpected power outage, or bitterly cold temperatures might reach areas that do not usually experience them.

That is what happened in February 2023 when a mass of Arctic air swept down through Canada and into the northeastern United States. It was the coldest air New Englanders had experienced in decades, and it came with equally bitter winds. Record-low temperatures were recorded in Boston, Massachusetts, and Albany, New York. At the top of New Hampshire's Mount Washington, the windchill reached a staggering −108 degrees Fahrenheit (−78°C).[5]

New England's experience was extreme, yet it was not unheard of. Each winter, extreme cold from the Arctic makes its way into parts of North America, Europe, and Asia. This is due to fluctuations in the polar vortex. The polar vortex is a naturally occurring area of low pressure and cold air that circulates counterclockwise over both poles year-round. In the winter in the Northern Hemisphere, the polar vortex sometimes expands, sending its cold air to lower latitudes via the jet stream. While the South Pole also has a polar vortex, it does not expand into other areas as often.

In addition to sudden drops in temperature, winter storms bring additional dangers. Storms that come with snow, sleet, and high winds may not have extremely low temperatures, but they can still create power outages and strand motorists. These conditions reduce visibility, making it easier for people stuck outdoors to get lost.

Extreme cold conditions in populated areas outside of the Arctic and Antarctic regions are most common in the Northern Hemisphere, which is home to roughly 90 percent of the world's population and features larger landmasses than the Southern Hemisphere.[6] Large landmasses create their own cold temperature extremes, separate from any winter storm or Arctic blast. Bismarck, North Dakota, in

▼ In January and February of 2019, a polar vortex hit New York City, freezing a fountain and other water features in the area.

the middle of the North American continent, is located at a similar latitude to Bern, Switzerland. Yet the average low temperature in January in Bismarck is a chilly 2 degrees Fahrenheit (−17°C).[7] In contrast, Bern's average low in January is 26 degrees Fahrenheit (−3°C).[8]

BODIES BEWARE

Regardless of the cause, extreme cold becomes dangerous when it results in hypothermia. Over time, a human body exposed to cold temperatures begins to lose heat faster than the body can generate it. Cold becomes more deadly when combined with wind, moisture, or both. While most cases of hypothermia occur in very cold conditions, even temperatures as mild as 40 degrees Fahrenheit (4°C) can cause hypothermia if a person is wet.[9] Exhaustion and dehydration also put a body at higher risk of hypothermia.

Hypothermia is a progressive condition leading to an eventual collapse of both physical and mental health processes. For many people, the first sign of hypothermia

> You can't fight [the cold]. You either adjust and dress accordingly or you suffer.[10]
>
> —Resident of Yakutsk, Russia, where temperatures routinely drop below −40 degrees Fahrenheit (−40°C)

is shivering. Typically occurring when the body temperature drops below its normal level, shivering forces activity to warm up the body and protect its vital organs. However, shivering requires the body to expend more energy than it would otherwise. That more quickly uses up the energy needed to maintain other body systems.

Left untreated in cold conditions, the body will continue to lose heat. Symptoms will progress from shivering to feeling tired and experiencing mental impairment. Victims will experience disorientation, confusion, and a loss of thinking clarity. The mental confusion it causes means the victim may be completely unaware that their brain is not working the way it should. In addition, muscles become colder, making it harder to perform even simple tasks such as working a zipper.

Eventually, extreme hypothermia will cause the body to stop shivering. The pulse and breathing slow down, the skin turns blue, and eventually the person loses consciousness. Without treatment, hypothermia can claim a life in just hours.

The US Centers for Disease Control and Prevention has identified several groups of people at higher risk of hypothermia than the general population. One group is elderly adults who do not have enough food, clothing, or heating. People experiencing homelessness also are at greater risk, as well as babies and children in cold bedrooms. People who spend significant amounts of time outside, as well as people with mental or physical conditions or substance abuse issues, are also at higher risk of hypothermia.

> **EXTREME COLD IN THE ER**
>
> An oxygen-starved body at normal temperature develops irreversible brain damage in just minutes. Yet in a body chilled to 59 degrees Fahrenheit (15°C), that damage does not occur for about two hours.[12] Some emergency room (ER) doctors are using this unique defense mechanism to treat life-threatening injuries, including gunshot and stab wounds. By quickly cooling patients who have lost a lot of blood, surgeons have extra time to stabilize and treat their injuries.

"Most people can get away with going out in the cold if dressed appropriately, but very young toddlers, infants and the elderly have more difficulty regulating their [body] temperature," said Dr. Michael Richardson.[11]

FROSTBITE

Frostbite is another danger. This freezing of body tissue most commonly affects exposed skin such as the cheeks, chin, nose, ears, fingers, and toes. Frostbite is a special concern during times of dangerous windchills. At a windchill below

FROZEN BUT NOT DEAD

Minnesotan Jean Hilliard was 19 years old when an icy road sent her car into a ditch on a −20-degree-Fahrenheit (−29°C) night in 1980.[14] Believing she was close to a friend's home, Hilliard took off walking down the deserted country road to get help. Her friend found her in his front yard six hours later, frozen solid. Medical staff at the local hospital were unable even to get a needle into her frozen arm. Thinking she was dead, the staff used heating pads to warm her up. Hilliard lived, leaving the hospital with just a few blisters and some numbness in her toes.

−30 degrees Fahrenheit (−34°C), frostbite can happen to exposed skin in ten minutes.[13]

Signs of frostbite include the skin feeling numb or tingling. It may change color, becoming bluish or pale and waxy looking. Frostbitten body parts may begin to ache. Since frostbite can freeze live tissues, stopping blood flow to them, those tissues may die. In some instances, the dead tissue may need to be amputated.

WATCH OUT FOR WATER

Moisture plays a critical role in the dangers of extreme cold. Water on the human body can cool the body faster than air, so getting wet can be especially dangerous. It can be difficult to assess whether ice on a body of water is thick enough to safely walk on. A person who falls through ice can lose their muscle coordination in as little as two minutes and

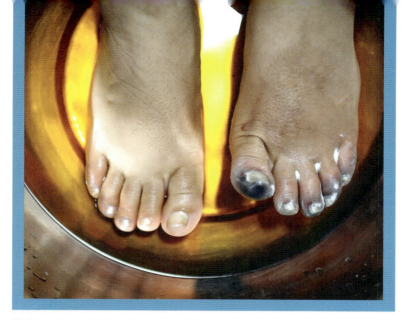

▲ People with frostbite should try to warm up and seek medical treatment right away.

can become unconscious in as little as 15 minutes.[15] A fall through the ice can quickly lead to drowning.

It also is important to remember that large bodies of water warm more slowly than land. It may be a warm summer day, yet a large lake in a northern climate might still be filled with 50-degree-Fahrenheit (10°C) water. Even in water at this temperature, a person can lose consciousness and drown in less than one hour.[16]

There are many dangers in the extreme cold. They can cause injury and even death. But some people have faced these dangers and lived to tell about them. Their stories offer important insights into what it takes to be an extreme cold survivor.

CHAPTER 3

THREE WEEKS IN ALASKA

Just more than a week after his cabin burned down, Steele had created a new shelter, heated by the same wood stove that had been the source of the fire. More than once, he scolded himself for putting a piece of cardboard in the stove, which likely led to the spark that had started his home fire. Now, he found himself needing to keep the stove going constantly just to take the edge off the extreme cold. The shelter wasn't ideal, but it was enough to keep him from freezing to death as temperatures reached −30 degrees Fahrenheit (−34°C).[1]

Even with the fire, Steele could see his breath. A bucket he urinated in when it was too cold to go

◀ Being able to build a fire is an especially important survival skill in cold environments.

▲ An image from video footage shows Steele with his SOS sign.

outside would freeze if it was even a few feet away from the stove. Perhaps worst of all, Steele suffered from a near-constant fear of another disastrous fire. "I would wake up unceasingly, every three hours, in a complete panic. . . . I was just thinking it was starting all over again."[2]

To improve his chances for rescue, he stomped the letters *SOS*, a universal distress signal, in the snow. He added ashes from the fire and the stove to make it stand out against the white landscape. As the days went on and more snow fell, Steele had to add more ash and continue to stomp out his distress signal. He told himself that if no one had rescued him by the time his food ran out, he would have to set out on foot through the snow to get help.

If it came to that, he was not sure where to go. He was surrounded by forests, lakes, rivers, and hills. Steele had purchased the property only a few months earlier. He didn't have a map, and he didn't yet know the area very well. He had arrived by air service, but now he had no way of contacting them or anyone else for help. There was a chance he would not survive.

THE ORIGINS OF SOS

The international distress code SOS has its roots in Morse code, a system of short pulses (dots) and long pulses (dashes) that represent letters and numbers. In Morse code, named after telegraph inventor Samuel Morse, SOS is transmitted with three short bursts, then three long ones, then three short ones. SOS as a standard distress call originated in 1906 at the International Radiotelegraph Convention, when delegates agreed on its short, fast format as an easy and consistent way to seek help. The letters *SOS* subsequently became another way to signal distress, especially for viewing from the air.

MAKING DO

As the days wore on, Steele continued to keep his fire going. He looked for additional supplies in the ruins of the cabin and added to his shelter as he could. He intentionally took his time so he would avoid injury.

On day ten, he found a container of coffee. Despite the coffee being charred from the fire, Steele found it raised his spirits and his energy level. He was able to incorporate the coffee into his regular routine, which also helped with his mental health. "Every morning when I made my coffee, I would grab a little piece of chalk I found in the shed and I'd write the mark of the day . . . and say, 'Welcome to the world, Day 15. . . . You've made it 15 days, you can make another 15 days.'"³

ANOTHER ALASKAN SURVIVOR

In December 1943, World War II (1939–1945) pilot Leon Crane's plane crashed during a routine test flight in Alaska. Crane parachuted to safety, the only survivor among five crew members. He landed in hip-deep snow in −40-degree-Fahrenheit (−40°C) temperatures with two packs of matches, a knife, and his parachute.⁴ As Crane began following a river north to find help, he discovered a well-stocked trapper's cabin. The supplies from that building helped the pilot return to his airfield near Fairbanks more than 80 days later.

The improved shelter was slightly warmer, though it was still very cold. Steele remembers that the coldest day was day 17. When he used the bathroom, his urine froze in the bucket in minutes. That day was the hardest for him mentally. He found himself thinking he wouldn't mind if he went to sleep and never woke up.

To fight that feeling, he set out the following day to walk to a lake a few miles away. The journey was anything but easy. With no snowshoes, he felt like he was swimming in the deep snow he navigated along the way. It took several days to get to the lake, where he cut holes in the ice to see if he could catch some fish. He also made signs for where an airplane could land, should someone come to rescue him.

Steele recalled that the difficult journey to the lake was a turning point for him. He had started to limp because of an old injury. He heard wolves nearby, and there was a moose that blocked his path for a while. He decided to make up a silly song about the moose, and he sang as he went along the path.

Another moose encounter also brought him joy back at his camp. "There was a moose that came right up to my shelter, and if it wanted to be violent, it could just easily tear everything down," he recalled. "It stamped my SOS . . . signal in the snow, totally destroyed it, and I just looked at it thinking, 'Man, I'm so hungry, you look tasty.'"[5]

> "I didn't have a map and I knew I didn't have enough knowledge of the whereabouts. I could have said 'oh, [let's go] that direction.' But I have no idea what waterways stay frozen enough for me to walk through—I could fall through the ice.[6]"
>
> —Tyson Steele, 2020

▲ Steele, *left*, was rescued by tactical flight officer Zac Johnson, *right*, and pilot Cliff Gilliland of the Alaska State Troopers.

Steele recalled staring at the moose for several minutes, marveling at how beautiful it was.

FINDING THE BEAUTY

Finding beauty and joy became as key to Steele's survival as food and shelter. "Things were beautiful all around me. There was northern lights several nights, shimmering greens and yellow and pinks. It was stunning. And even the wolves though they were scary, they were beautiful." He added, "A full moon one night, there was just beauty all around me and it helped me be happy amidst all the tragedy."[7]

On January 9, 2020, three weeks after the fire, Steele was fixing a breakfast of burnt oatmeal and brown sugar when he heard the helicopter. His parents had become concerned when they did not hear from him. They contacted the pilot

Steele usually worked with, who suggested contacting the Alaska State Troopers to do a welfare check on him. Racing outside his shelter, Steele waved his arms over his head. He pointed to his airstrip and soon found himself face-to-face with the first person he'd seen in months.

Meanwhile, his rescuers were pleasantly surprised. While the young man had lost some 20 pounds (9 kg) during his ordeal, he was in good health.[8] In addition, he seemed mentally healthy. The troopers noted that in other situations, they had found people who had been lost for only a couple of days who were experiencing extreme mental distress. Steele's only request of his rescuers as they flew away from the site of his ordeal was to get a breakfast sandwich and coffee at a fast-food chain.

THE KID WHO SLEPT OUTSIDE

Like Tyson Steele, Isaac Ortman discovered a passion for the outdoors at a young age. In early 2023, the Duluth teenager recorded his 1,000th night of sleeping outside, including in temperatures below −20 degrees Fahrenheit (−29°C).[9] Ortman began sleeping outdoors in April 2020 during the COVID-19 pandemic. Then, it simply stuck. For cold nights, Ortman puts quilts in the bottom of his hammock for additional insulation, and sometimes he adds a hot water bottle in addition to wearing long underwear inside his down sleeping bag beneath two down quilts.

CHAPTER 4

ABANDONED IN
THE ARCTIC

In the second half of the 1800s, some scientists began to theorize that the polar regions held the key to understanding weather and climate. To test that theory, a group of ten nations agreed to set up 13 stations around the Arctic to collect data on weather, magnetic activity, and celestial objects.[1]

The United States contributed a team of 22 men, including the leader, US Army lieutenant Adolphus Greely. A surgeon and two Inuit hunters later joined the group, which was charged with setting up the northernmost of these stations. The expedition began in July 1881 with the successful establishment of an Arctic exploration camp situated on Lady Franklin Bay

◀ Adolphus Greely was born in 1844 in Massachusetts and joined the army at 17 years old.

▲ An illustration from 1884 depicted the members of the Greely Expedition.

in Nunavut, Canada. The camp, named Fort Conger, was just 500 miles (805 km) from the North Pole.[2]

The first year of the expedition went smoothly. The summer of 1881 was unusually warm, meaning the expedition encountered few challenges with the ice that usually made sea travel in the area unpredictable. The soldiers set up stations to monitor weather conditions. They constructed a spacious winter house with bunks, offices, dining tables, two coal-burning stoves, and a kitchen range. Fort Conger's winter house sat near a vein of coal, which would provide fuel for the expedition's heating and cooking needs in a land where wood was scarce.

Game in the area was plentiful, with the hunters providing musk oxen, caribou, and ducks to supplement the rations within the expedition's 350 short tons (320 metric tons) of supplies.[3] Unlike most Arctic expeditions, this one was not left with a ship capable of transporting the full team or meeting another ship to transfer supplies. Instead, the expedition had just a small coal-powered steamer. In addition, few of the expedition members had any experience on the sea or in the Arctic.

The original expedition plan included a resupply by ship in the summer of 1882 and a departure in September 1883. Understanding the challenges of Arctic conditions, planners sent three years of supplies just in case. Even with abundant supplies, the long nights during the six-month winter proved a challenge for the crew. Extreme cold and darkness outside meant the expedition crew had to spend extended amounts of time inside the winter house. Many resorted to journaling and gossip to pass the time.

FARTHEST NORTH

Late February 1882 brought sunlight for the first time since October and a new

FORT CONGER

After being abandoned by the Greely Expedition, Fort Conger got a second life as a base for polar explorations led by American explorer Robert Peary in 1898. Peary used wood from the original Fort Conger structure to build a series of smaller, interconnected structures based on Inuit designs that were easier to heat. Learning from the past, Peary also used large sleds to transport supplies rather than relying on ships. Fort Conger was formally recognized for its significance in 1978 and remains a Polar Heritage Site.

opportunity for exploration. The team decided to take advantage of its location to claim for the United States a new record for the farthest-north expedition, beating the previous record held by the United Kingdom. It was early in the season, and the first attempt was blocked by ice, but a small team was able to reach a latitude of 83 degrees, two minutes, and eight seconds.[4]

The accomplishment broke the previous 1607 record by several miles. The team returned to Fort Conger on July 1, 1882. It joined the other members of the expedition in watching the horizon, where they hoped to soon spot a ship carrying fresh supplies and letters from home.

By August, Greely realized no supplies were coming. Unknown to the team, a supply ship did attempt a drop-off, but it was stopped by ice. The crew of the resupply ship unloaded a portion of their supplies in caches some 250 miles (400 km) from Fort Conger.[5] While Greely and his men were disappointed, they had extra supplies with them. They resigned themselves to waiting out another long, dark winter, hoping their supplies held out.

As before, the extended darkness, extreme cold, and lack of activity took a toll on the team's morale. Despite that, the expedition continued to log the weather data it had come

▲ The 1893 World's Columbian Exposition in Chicago included a diorama of the Greely Expedition.

to collect. Each day, the team made 500 measurements, including wind speed and temperature. "Thermometer range from –44.0 to –56.4 [degrees Fahrenheit (–42.2 to –49.1°C)], observed and corrected," stated one log entry. Another read, "A still lower temperature today, from –47.2 to –57.2 [degrees Fahrenheit (–44 to –49.6°C)]."[6]

The summer of 1883 brought sunlight but little else. Once again, the team received no restock of supplies.

This time, the ice sent the supply ship to the bottom of the sea, along with most of the supplies intended for the expedition. As the summer wore on and no ships appeared, the expedition team's worst fears were realized. There was no help coming, and if the men wanted to survive, it would be up to them.

Following the original expedition plan, Greely informed the team members that they would need to leave Fort Conger and travel the treacherous 250 miles (400 km) south to find supplies and a ride back home at Cape Sabine in Nunavut. On August 9, 1883, the team left the relative comfort of Fort Conger and loaded only food, survival gear, and their precious scientific records into their 28-foot (8.5 m) steamboat and some small wooden boats for the long and challenging ride.[7]

The expedition team was only two weeks gone from Fort Conger when its steamboat became trapped in ice.

INVALUABLE DATA

The Greely Expedition's contribution to meteorological knowledge remains relevant even in modern times. The data gathered by the expedition members is generating new interest as climate scientists seek to better understand how the climate is changing, especially in the polar regions. Thanks to the efforts of Greely and his team, modern scientists have a comprehensive baseline of Arctic weather data to compare with contemporary readings and measurements.

Reluctantly, the group agreed to Greely's plan to transfer their items, including the two remaining boats, to an ice floe and take their chances with the sea and winds. Trapped on the floating ice, the men had barely enough room to stay out of the water and no control over their destination. It felt like a miracle when they finally landed south of Cape Sabine at what is now called Arviat after 51 days on the water. They named their new outpost Camp Clay.

HANGING ON

Arviat was rocky, windswept, and even more inhospitable than the area around Fort Conger. There was little, if any, wildlife to hunt and little vegetation other than moss. Greely oversaw the building of a makeshift shelter constructed from rock, ice, and moss. He sent small groups of his men on expeditions to find caches of supplies left by earlier efforts or by other exploration teams.

Greely, like the others, believed a rescue party was waiting for them in nearby Greenland, and in early spring, they would be saved. "The party are in very high spirit, feeling certain we can get through," he wrote. "I, however, am fully aware of the very dangerous situation we are yet in. I am determined to make our food last until April 1st."[8]

A small team sent north to Cape Sabine came back with mixed news. They had found written records from the teams of both the 1882 and 1883 supply attempts, which detailed the failure of their missions. However, the notes also mentioned three small stores of food totaling 1,300 rations, about enough food for 25 people for a few weeks.[9]

The promise of rations was enticing. The expedition currently had only enough rations for approximately 35 days, and only in meager portions: ten ounces (283 g) of bread, one pound (0.5 kg) of meat, and two ounces (57 g) of potatoes per day.[10] It was roughly half of the normal Arctic ration per US Army guidelines.

Greely made the decision to abandon Camp Clay and move the team to Cape Sabine and its cache of supplies before winter. Even with the possibility of more supplies, he was well aware of the challenge ahead.

CALORIES AND COLD

Hunger and hypothermia are closely related. Cold conditions require the body to expend more energy to maintain a normal body temperature. Polar activities, such as traveling by dogsled, require even more energy. An adult who normally needs 2,000 to 2,500 calories a day might need 6,500 to 8,000 calories for an active day in extremely cold conditions.[11] Modern polar adventurers favor foods that are high in fat and calories and low in moisture so they don't freeze, such as chocolate and nuts.

▲ Cape Sabine is on Pim Island. The remains of the walls that the Greely Expedition constructed on Cape Sabine were still visible more than a century later.

"I . . . foresee a winter of starvation diet and probably deaths," he wrote. "Our fuel is so scanty that we are in danger of perishing on that score alone."[12]

It took four days of backbreaking work to relocate the camp to its new location on Cape Sabine. Once again, the team struggled to build a shelter using whatever materials were on hand. The team members built the new shelter from rocks and snow. The roof was an overturned boat they had found and dragged across the ice. The shelter was small—the men barely fit inside, and it was impossible to stand up. For warmth, the team had little more than robes and sleeping bags made from buffalo skin. While the bags could be warm, ice could collect in the buffalo hair, weighing them down and making them difficult to move and carry.

In their rush to look for caches of supplies before winter, team members drove themselves to exhaustion, with no food, water, or sleep. One member of the team froze both hands and both feet. He pleaded to be left to die, but his fellow team members refused. Instead of hauling back some food they had found, they hauled him back to the camp. The expedition members even agreed to accept a reduction in rations, giving their impaired colleague more to improve his chances of survival.

In one last effort before the sun departed and winter took over, Greely ordered the expedition's scientific records to be placed in a cairn several miles from their camp. A cairn is a pile of stones created to mark something of importance. In his personal journal, he wrote, "I am determined that our work shall not perish with us."[13]

WAITING TO DIE

With fuel and food scarce, the expedition cooks had to limit their fires to warm what food they had. Sometimes they burned parts of barrels or seal blubber. With no material for a chimney, expedition members hid their heads in their sleeping bags to avoid the smoke in the enclosed shelter. The men experienced dehydration because they were unable to use precious fuel to melt ice into drinking water.

The deaths from starvation and scurvy began in January 1884. As spring approached, the team was able to kill a handful of birds and harvest tiny crustaceans that could be eaten. Yet these new

> If you drop a mitten and lose your mitten for five minutes, you're likely going to lose your hand. Everything is heightened.[14]
>
> —Buddy Levy, author of Labyrinth of Ice, *on the temperatures the Greely Expedition faced*

▲ A photo was taken of the six survivors, including Julius Frederick, Maurice Connell, and Francis Long, *back row*, and Henry Biederbick, Adolphus Greely, and David Brainard, *front row*.

food sources were far from enough, and five men died in April, followed by another four in May. Greely wrote in his journal about learning to notice the mental breakdown that typically preceded the deaths.

By the time the Arctic summer arrived, men had resorted to eating shoes, candle wax, and even bird droppings. There were signs that some of the living members of the expedition were cutting chunks of flesh off of the recently deceased. One team member was executed for consistently stealing food from what limited rations remained.

As her husband and his crew withered away from starvation, Greely's wife, Henrietta, had been working tirelessly to secure his rescue. Having exhausted every military connection she had, Henrietta Greely used the popular press and the resulting public outrage over the abandonment of the Greely Expedition to force Congress to approve a rescue expedition. The rescue expedition left New York on April 23, 1884, under the command of Winfield Schley.

Schley and his crew arrived at Cape Sabine on June 22, 1884, to find just seven expedition members, all soldiers, still alive. One of the seven died on the rescue ship. The remaining six survivors, including Greely, arrived back in the United States on August 1, 1884. While initially regarded as heroes, subsequent allegations of cannibalism cast a shadow over the survivors, sending their considerable scientific accomplishments into near obscurity.

CHAPTER 5

HEROINE OF WRANGEL ISLAND

Ada Delutuk Blackjack was no stranger to challenges. She was born north of the Arctic Circle in May 1898 in the remote Spruce Creek village in Alaska. She was a member of the Iñupiaq people, who are indigenous to the area.

Blackjack's father died of food poisoning when she was just eight years old, which led her mother to send Ada and one of her sisters to live in a missionary school in Nome, Alaska. Ada learned to speak, read, and write English at the school. She also learned how to cook and sew, including sewing animal furs into the garments required to survive Alaska winters. But she

◀ Ada Blackjack went on an Arctic voyage in order to provide for her young son.

THE CANINE HEROES OF NOME

In January 1925, Nome was ravaged by diphtheria, an often-fatal respiratory disease. The closest supply of critical medicine was 674 miles (1,085 km) away.[1] The only hope to transport the medicine was by dogsled. Twenty drivers and 150 dogs completed legs of a harrowing five-and-a-half-day sled dog relay.[2] Temperatures reached −85 degrees Fahrenheit (−65°C).[3] Four dogs died, and lead dogs Togo and Balto went on to win international recognition for extreme cold survival.

missed out on learning many of the survival skills that were typically passed on to children in Iñupiaq villages.

At age 16, Ada married a dogsled driver named Jack Blackjack. The two moved to Alaska's Seward Peninsula and had three children. Ada Blackjack realized early in the relationship that her new husband was abusive. He hit her and sometimes denied her food. She stayed with him for the sake of their children, two of whom had died at an early age.

Her only remaining child, Bennett, developed tuberculosis around the age of five. Tuberculosis is an airborne disease caused by bacteria. It was a common and serious disease at that time in Alaska. A diagnosis of tuberculosis was challenging. Treating the disease required special care as well as the isolation of those who had it to prevent them from spreading it to others.

Around the time Bennett became sick, Jack deserted his wife and son, forcing them to walk the 40 miles (64 km) from their home on the Seward Peninsula back to Nome.[4] Arriving in Nome with no husband and no support, Blackjack had little choice but to surrender Bennett to an orphanage that accepted children whose parents, while still alive, were unable to care for them. Then she set about finding work that would pay enough for her to eventually get her son back.

$50 A MONTH

Blackjack was working as a house cleaner when an acquaintance told her about an expedition that was forming to go to Wrangel Island. This is a remote Arctic island north of Siberia, about 600 miles (970 km) from Nome.[5] Expedition members were seeking natives of Alaska to travel with them. They needed native people who knew how to sew warm clothing from animal hides and who could speak English. The pay was $50 a month, which is equivalent to about $800 in modern times.[6] The expedition would be led by a 20-year-old Canadian named Allan Crawford. Three other young men—Errol Lorne Knight, Frederick Maurer, and Milton Galle—were the other expedition members.

▲ Ada Blackjack, *center*, joined four men on the expedition to Wrangel Island. The team also brought along a cat named Victoria.

By the time the expedition departed on September 9, 1921, Blackjack was the only native Alaskan still willing to go on the trip. She was uncomfortable being the only woman with a group of four men. The men told her they planned to recruit more Indigenous expedition members when they stopped in Siberia on the way to Wrangel Island. Blackjack believed them and joined the expedition, which arrived on Wrangel Island one week later on September 15, 1921. While the ship had stopped in Siberia as planned, no other Indigenous expedition members were recruited.

Blackjack was unaware of the true nature of the planned, two-year expedition. It was organized by a Canadian man,

Vilhjalmur Stefansson, an explorer whose given name was William Stevenson and who wanted to gain money and fame by showing that the Arctic was a good place to live. In reality, Stefansson had dreams of taking Wrangel Island from Russia and making it part of Canada. He arranged for just six months of supplies because he believed and wanted to prove that people could live off the land on the island by hunting foxes, seals, and polar bears.[7] He also said he planned to send more supplies the following summer.

Blackjack had second thoughts as she surveyed the desolate island, where the soil remained frozen all year. Wrangel Island has a large

POLAR BEARS

Wrangel Island is known for having the world's highest concentration of polar bear dens. The estimated 3,000 polar bears of the region divide their time between the nearby sea ice and land in Russia and the United States.[8] As the largest land predator, the polar bear makes a formidable enemy for unwary travelers. Bear behavior experts suggest travelers in areas inhabited by polar bears avoid contact if at all possible and carry bear spray at all times.

population of polar bears, and Blackjack had struggled since childhood with a fear of polar bears. She considered seeking a ride back to Nome on the same ship that had dropped her and the other expedition members off. However, she had made a promise and intended to keep it.

AN UNEASY START

The expedition team arrived on Wrangel Island late in the summer, adding a sense of urgency to their first few weeks. The four men focused on building shelters from tents and sod, using several wood-burning stoves they brought along for warmth. Blackjack began sewing skins the team had brought with them into coats, leggings, and boots. The team did not focus on hunting and storing meat, thinking the hunting would be robust all year long.

Within several weeks, Blackjack had a growing uneasiness with the barren surroundings on the island, and her homesickness increased in intensity. Despite her fear

▼ Wrangel Island has an area of about 2,800 square miles (7,300 sq km). The island is mostly low-lying tundra, though it has some mountains.

of polar bears, she began wandering away from the camp alone. Other times, the expedition members found her crying. Even though Blackjack spoke English, the four men did not share their daily plans for activities with her, leading her to feel even more isolated. Even worse, they sometimes denied her food or forced her to remain outside to punish her when they thought she was not working hard enough.

Over time, Blackjack and the other expedition members began to settle into more of a routine. Life on the island started to go more smoothly, despite frequent storms and winter temperatures at times reaching −52 degrees Fahrenheit (−47°C).[9] Blackjack celebrated her 24th birthday on the island on May 10, 1922.[10] All of the expedition members were looking forward to the arrival of the supply ship that summer, which would also offer an opportunity to return to Nome. However, ice and storms prevented the supply ship from reaching them. By September, the team members had to face the prospect of another winter on the island alone.

DARKNESS AND HUNGER

With no new supplies, the expedition team found itself under greater pressure to prepare for another long

Arctic winter. Unlike before, the members began to work harder at storing meat from their hunts for the future. They also began to ration food, including for their sled dogs. The team started to notice signs of scurvy, a disease caused by a lack of vitamin C, which is present in plants such as citrus fruits, tomatoes, and potatoes—foods the expedition did not have. Red meat has vitamin C but only in its raw, or rare, form.

By late December, the team was surviving on hard bread, seal oil, and walrus skin. By January, they were making plans for a dangerous attempt to get help by crossing the sea ice to Siberia. It would be a 100-mile (160 km) journey on foot and dogsled, mostly in the dark. Storms would be frequent and the cold intense. In early January, Crawford and Knight attempted the trek and were forced to turn back after 13 days due to Knight's poor health and their dogs' weakness from lack of food. In late January, Maurer, Galle, and Crawford made another attempt to cross the ice with the dogs, leaving Blackjack and Knight behind. The temperature was −50 degrees Fahrenheit (−46°C).[11]

Journal entries from expedition members noted that they agreed to send three people instead of two due to the shortage of food at camp. They promised Blackjack and

▲ **Wrangel Island lies in the Chukchi Sea, which is covered in sea ice during winter.**

Knight that they would send help as soon as possible. Even if everything went well, it would be months before any help could arrive. But Crawford, Maurer, and Galle were never seen again.

Blackjack soon found herself in the position of hunter, trapper, nursemaid, and cook for an increasingly ill and frequently verbally abusive Knight. She was forced to keep the camp going all on her own and go outside alone in all conditions, despite her fear of polar bears. Knight, now very ill with scurvy, was confined to his cot. If the two were to survive, it would be up to Blackjack alone.

SMALL VICTORIES

Blackjack gave most of the red meat she caught to Knight in an attempt to keep him alive. Yet as the winter wore on, she too began to develop symptoms of scurvy as well as snow blindness, which limited her ability to trap wildlife. In June, she taught herself how to use a rifle to shoot waterfowl that were returning to the island. She also dragged a giant piece of driftwood she found on the beach to the camp for firewood.

> That strength and survival that [Blackjack] showed, doing what you can and figuring things out, those are things that all of us have to have to survive.[12]
>
> —Holly Mititquq Nordlum, producer of a documentary about Ada Blackjack

Knight died of scurvy in late June 1923, leaving Blackjack completely alone on the island. Too weak from hunger to bury his body, she surrounded it with boxes to keep it safe from wild animals. She then moved herself to a supply tent and built a stove there from cans she had hammered together. She used pieces of driftwood, canvas, and skins to build herself a small boat so she could hunt seals on the water.

Blackjack had just opened the last box of biscuits from the expedition's supplies on August 20, 1923, when she heard a noise. It was the foghorn of the ship sent to rescue the expedition members and return them to Nome. The rescue, under the direction of Stefansson's colleague, Harold Noice, had expected to depart the island with five people. He found only Blackjack alive and returned her to Nome, where she was reunited with her son. While Blackjack never received all the wages she was due, she was able to have her son treated for his tuberculosis in Seattle, Washington.

SNOW BLINDNESS

Ultraviolet rays from sunlight reflecting off snow and ice can cause damage to the eyes. This condition, called snow blindness, is especially common in polar areas, though it also can happen when sunlight is reflected off water or sand. Extreme cold also can cause eye problems by either freezing or drying out the surface of the eye, called the cornea. People engaging in outdoor activities including hiking, skiing, and riding snowmobiles should be sure to include protective eyewear in their preparations.

CHAPTER 6

MIRACLE IN THE YUKON

Twenty-year-old Helen Klaben set out from her native Brooklyn, New York, in the summer of 1962 on a road trip to see the world. She ended up in Fairbanks, Alaska, where she stayed for about six months. For her next adventure, she wanted to explore the San Francisco, California, area. However, it was thousands of miles away through heavily forested and often bitterly cold wilderness. When she heard an ad on the local radio station placed by a pilot seeking a passenger to share costs on a flight to California, she jumped at the chance.

The ad was placed by Ralph Flores, a 41-year-old Mexican immigrant and former boxer who was

◀ The Yukon remains one of the most sparsely populated areas in the world.

▲ Helen Klaben was adventurous and self-reliant from the time she was a child. As a young adult, she was eager to travel.

working as an electrician. Flores lived in the San Francisco area, but he was working on a project on Alaska's North Slope. An amateur pilot, his five-seater airplane allowed him to see his wife and five children when he had the occasional day off. He was happy to have Klaben share the cost of the fuel for the trip, which began in early February 1963. They started with a hop from Fairbanks to Whitehorse, Canada, where they refueled the plane.

The duo ended up spending three days stuck in Whitehorse due to stormy weather. It was still stormy and −43 degrees Fahrenheit (−42°C) when Flores took off on February 4. He filed a flight plan for an arrival 600 miles (970 km) away in Fort Saint John, Canada.[1]

After hours of battling snow and strong winds, Flores tried flying above the clouds to determine where he was and then descending to follow the Alaska Highway to Fort Saint John. Without sufficient experience flying with instruments, Flores was unable to get his bearings. He accidentally switched the engine to an empty fuel tank and was unable to switch it to a full one in time to restart the engine.

Their small plane lost altitude until it crashed into a forest of spruce trees near the border of the Yukon Territory and British Columbia. Flores watched the right wingtip

> ## THE YUKON
> The Yukon is one of three Canadian territories and shares borders with Alaska as well as Canada's British Columbia province and Northwest Territories. It is home to Canada's highest mountain as well as its largest ice field and the westernmost point in Canada. Fewer than 35,000 people live in the Yukon, which is roughly the same size as the country of Spain.[4] The Arctic Circle also passes through the Yukon.

hit the trees. He closed his eyes as everything suddenly went black.

ALIVE

The crash left both Flores and Klaben alive but unconscious. When Klaben awoke, she realized she was in a crashed plane but had no idea how long she had been there. She realized her left arm was broken, and her right foot was stuck between the seat and the side of the plane. A cut on her chin had dripped blood on a map in her lap. Flores, she quickly saw, was likewise bloody from cuts on his face and head. The plane's thermometer read −48 degrees Fahrenheit (−44°C).[2] It was so cold their blood was freezing, holding the injured tissues in place.

Eventually, Flores and Klaben were able to exit the plane and assess their situation. They had crashed into the side of a heavily forested mountain, in snow that reached five feet (1.5 m) deep in places.[3] They had no sleeping bags to stay warm, no axe to chop firewood, and no rifle to hunt

▲ Flores's plane was badly mangled in the crash. It landed near Watson Lake.

wild game. They had matches and fuel from the airplane, a screwdriver, a hammer, and a hunting knife. For food, they had just four cans of sardines, two cans each of fruit cocktail and tuna, a box of crackers, some chocolate, and some vitamin pills.

Flores knew the airport at Fort Saint John would report that they never arrived. That would lead to a search of the area in their flight path. The two began to use what they could find to turn the crashed plane into a shelter that could help them survive the bitter cold. They set up a makeshift camp inside the plane and used tree boughs to try to stuff holes in the wreckage. They located two mirrors and had them ready to signal when the search planes arrived. Flores worked to make sure that the numbers on the plane's tail were as visible as possible to help rescuers identify it.

> **I thought we were going to die. . . . It was very cold and it was long and dark.**[5]
>
> —Helen Klaben, recalling the ordeal in 1996

Flores had suffered cracked ribs, head wounds, and a broken jaw. Klaben's fingers had begun to freeze as she lay unconscious in the wreckage after the crash. Her feet also froze, making it difficult for her to move around. To prevent further damage, the two wrapped her sweaters around their feet and covered them with pieces of canvas from the plane.

With both believing they would be quickly found by searchers, they did not plan ahead and ration what little food they had. The food was gone within ten days. After the food ran out, they used an empty oil can to melt snow and drink the warm water. They drank large amounts of water, pretending it was soup or another satisfying meal. When Klaben realized she had a tube of toothpaste in her luggage, they squeezed the toothpaste out, melted it in water, and drank it as food.

Flores and Klaben were freezing cold and in pain. They spent their days huddled around the fire, sheltering in the plane. They talked about food and read from Flores' Bible or from some of the books Klaben had brought along on

ANATOMY OF A SEARCH

Most search and rescue missions follow a similar protocol, beginning with the initial missing persons call. Once a person is confirmed missing and available details are gathered, searchers make guesses as to what might have happened. That allows search teams to place people where they are most likely to encounter the lost person. Weather permitting, searches typically go for as long as a missing person is presumed to be alive. Likelihood of survival is calculated by how many people typically die after a certain time in the terrain and conditions in question.

her travels. Although they heard planes fly overhead, they remained unseen due to heavy tree cover above their crash site.

LAST-DITCH ATTEMPT

From time to time, Flores and Klaben could hear a faint noise in the distance that sounded like a chainsaw or a sawmill. As the days dragged on and some of their injuries healed, Flores began to plan an expedition beyond the crash site. He fashioned snowshoes from wire and tree branches and set out to find the noise.

Flores spent several days away from the camp, building and sleeping in shelters made of snow mounds on the nights he was gone. He found a pond several miles from their plane and stomped SOS in the snow, along with an arrow pointing to their crash site. The letters were roughly 75 feet (23 m) tall to make them visible from the sky.[6]

Flores then returned to the plane, and together with Klaben, he built a makeshift sled from plane wreckage. They used this sled to haul their few supplies to a new campsite. That site, located in a more open area, would be more visible to people searching by air. Using a tarp and cushions from the plane, they set up a new camp. By this time, Klaben had

▲ Helen Klaben, *pictured*, and Flores left their original camp and built a new camp with a tarp and a few other supplies.

learned to throw tree boughs on the fire when planes flew over to increase their odds of being seen.

On March 24, 1963, a bush pilot was flying supplies to a hunting outfitter's business in the area when another person in the plane saw the SOS. The crew then spotted Flores out walking. Following the arrow, they flew over the plane wreckage and identified it as Flores's craft by its serial number. The following day, a second plane flew a rescue team to the same site and was able to land on a frozen pond. The crew found Flores and then Klaben by following Flores' tracks in the snow. It had been nearly 50 days since the crash.

> **They were really quite a strange-looking pair. He had 50 days of beard growth and got off the plane with his belt tightened around his waist. She looked like a young socialite—with cardigans wrapped around her feet.[8]**
>
> —Bob Hill, journalist, 1963, on how Flores and Klaben looked when rescued

What they found was both shocking and amazing. The survivors were severely malnourished. Flores had lost 57 pounds (26 kg). Klaben had lost 40 pounds (18 kg).[7] When offered food, Klaben said she was not hungry and had to force herself to eat. Weak and with frozen feet, Klaben had to be carried out of the camp by the rescue team. Some of the toes on Klaben's right foot had to be amputated due to frostbite, and Flores required oral surgery for his broken jaw. Yet the two had survived with virtually no food or emergency supplies in the extreme cold of a Yukon winter.

Flores and Klaben's miraculous survival story quickly made headlines. As the survivors recovered in the Whitehorse General Hospital, they learned that Flores' 16-year-old daughter had written a letter to President John F. Kennedy pleading for the government to help search for her father. After Flores was found, the White House sent her a letter. "As I know you are," the White House letter stated, "we are most happy that miraculous happenings as this sometimes do occur."[9]

SURVIVING WITHOUT FOOD

Human bodies evolved to survive multiple physical challenges, including reduced caloric intake for extended periods. While humans can survive only minutes without oxygen and a few days without water, humans have been known to survive without food for more than a month. In the absence of food, the body switches from relying on dietary sugars to glycogen, which is stored in the liver and muscles. Once glycogen is depleted, the body begins to access energy available in the body's fat stores. The final source of energy to be accessed is protein, which is primarily found in muscles.

CHAPTER 7

AGAINST INCREDIBLE ODDS

The early 1900s saw adventurers around the world seeking to become the first to reach the South Pole. Irishman Ernest Shackleton was among them. But after failing to be the first to reach the South Pole when Roald Amundsen beat him to it in 1911, Shackleton decided to mount an expedition to become the first to cross the vast, uncharted landmass of Antarctica. He called it the Imperial Trans-Antarctic Expedition.

Shackleton devised an ambitious plan that would involve two ships. One ship, the *Aurora*, would head to the Ross Sea and send a team overland to leave caches of supplies for the expedition. The expedition

◀ The Weddell Sea has a lot of ice for most of the year, which stopped many early expeditions to the area.

would use these supplies on its journey from the South Pole back to the Ross Sea coast. The other ship, the *Endurance*, would head to the Weddell Sea, where the expedition would make landfall and cross the continent. The *Endurance* had been built for polar voyages, with a keel measuring more than seven feet (2 m) thick and a coal-fired steam engine.[1] The builder, which specialized in ships for hunting whales

▼ Ernest Shackleton had many loyal crewmembers who accompanied him on multiple voyages.

and seals, designed and built the *Endurance* for maximum strength in challenging, icy conditions.

Shackleton boarded the *Endurance* in Buenos Aires, Argentina, in October 1914. Together with 27 crew members and 69 dogs, he set sail for South Georgia island.[2] On the way, they realized one additional sailor had stowed away, bringing the crew total to 28. In November 1914, the *Endurance* arrived at a whaling station on South Georgia to some worrying news. There, ship captains were reporting unusually bad ice conditions.

Some experienced sailors doubted that the *Endurance* would be able to get through the ice. The ice reports caused Shackleton to delay the expedition's departure in the hopes that the ice situation would improve. He also ordered extra provisions, including extra coal to fuel the engine. Finally, the *Endurance* left the whaling station on December 4.

Within two days of its departure, the *Endurance* encountered the pack ice that surrounds the continent of Antarctica. The ship was able to slowly pick its way through the ice floes. On January 18, 1915, the ship was within one day's sail of its destination on land when the wind picked up and jammed the ice floes together, trapping the *Endurance* within them. The ship could no longer navigate. It had instead become a part of the shifting ice, subject to moving with the ice pack whether it was going in the desired direction or not.

TRAPPED

With the Antarctic winter on the horizon and no way out of the ice, Shackleton quickly informed the crew that they would be delayed on their expedition and that they needed to settle in and wait things out. Crew members did what they could to free the ship as temperatures dropped to −4 degrees Fahrenheit (−20°C).[3] Their efforts were in vain, however, and the *Endurance* remained a captive of the ice for ten months. Shackleton oversaw the day-to-day work, trying to maintain efficient operations while also keeping morale and spirits high during the extended darkness of the Antarctic winter. Crew members began calling the hold of the ship the Ritz after the fancy hotel of the same name. They made up special activities and held parties to pass the time. When there was light, the crew went outside on the ice floe and played hockey and football.

The effect the ice floe could have on the ship was a constant concern. While many hoped the arrival of spring would free the ship from the ice, others feared it was only a matter of time until the pressure of the ice on the ship became too much. That fear became reality on October 23, 1915, when the pressure of the ice twisted the ship's stern post, creating a leak. Despite ongoing efforts by the crew to relieve some of the pressure, the ice continued to press on the ship. Shackleton made the call to abandon the *Endurance* on October 27.

Crew members unloaded as much as they could from the ship before it buckled completely. Cracks developing in the ice around the ship forced the expedition to set up operations more than one mile (1.6 km) away, in what they termed Ocean Camp.[4] At that point, they could only wait as the ice continued its assault on the ship, finally sinking it on November 21. As they watched it sink, Shackleton said to his crew, "She's going, boys!"[5] The expedition was now afloat on an ice floe with

ENDURANCE DISCOVERED

The heroic story of the Imperial Trans-Antarctic Expedition made news headlines in March 2022 when a team of marine archaeologists discovered the wreck of the *Endurance*. The ship was located almost two miles (3.2 km) below the surface of the sea. The frigid waters meant the wreck was in very good condition, with features including the ship's wheel, ropes, and portholes largely intact. The discovery came 100 years to the day after Ernest Shackleton's March 1922 burial on South Georgia island following his death there from a heart attack.[6]

only three small lifeboats and no means of communicating with the outside world. While the Antarctic summer was just around the corner, they were still hundreds of miles from land.

Shackleton quickly rallied the expedition members around a new mission of finding supplies on Paulet Island. He had ordered provisions to be sent there in preparation for the *Endurance*'s expedition. The crew loaded the lifeboats with what supplies remained and began the backbreaking work of hauling them across the ice. For five months, they wandered across the barren, icy landscape. Yet once again, the shifting ice pulled them away from their destination. Instead of heading west toward the island, they had floated east on the ice.

Shackleton quickly changed plans when the expedition saw Elephant Island in the distance. By this time, some of the ice had cleared, creating more open sea. The crew left the ice and launched the three lifeboats. After seven days of battling large waves in small boats, the crew members landed on the island. It was the first time in nearly 500 days that any of them had set foot on land.

Yet Elephant Island was desolate and uninhabited, with no supplies and no ships likely to pass by. Shackleton

▲ The expedition had an official photographer, Frank Hurley, who documented the challenges of the voyage, including when ice crushed the *Endurance*.

realized that to save his crew, he would have to make his way back to South Georgia island. That, however, was 800 miles (1,290 km) away, through the turbulent and unpredictable Weddell Sea.[7]

BIG WAVES, TINY BOAT

In late April, Shackleton selected five expedition members to join him in a desperate last attempt at a rescue. For this, they

▲ Shackleton and five expedition members departed in a single small lifeboat. They traveled 60 to 70 miles (97–113 km) per day.

chose one of the lifeboats, the *James Caird*, which was just 22.5 feet (6.9 m) long.[8] The crew staying on Elephant Island created a shelter from rock walls, with the remaining two lifeboats turned upside down on top of the walls to form a roof. They used material from the *Endurance*'s old sails, along with tent fabric, mud, and snow, to make the shelter as windproof as possible, protecting them from the island's frequent blizzards. They had a small stove that could burn blubber for warmth and cooking. The crew ate whatever penguins they could catch and skin with their partially frostbitten hands.

The *James Caird* was launched in the early morning hours of April 24 as the wind at last calmed. In addition to its six occupants, the boat held provisions for six weeks at sea plus whatever extra warm clothing and reindeer sleeping bags the Elephant Island expedition members could spare. Perhaps most importantly, the crew packed two sextants and navigational tables and charts. Navigation would be critical to avoid being lost at sea, yet it relied on clear enough skies to see the sun—something that happened only infrequently between storms.

> "Everything deeply snowed over, footgear frozen so stiff that we could only put it on by degrees, not a dry or warm pair of gloves amongst us.[10]"
>
> —Alexander Macklin, physician on the expedition, journaling about Elephant Island

The team had done the best it could to stretch precious pieces of canvas over the open deck to keep out the waves, and a pump was on board to help remove water. Despite these preparations, worsening weather and heavy ice accumulation on the deck meant the crew had to bail water simply to keep afloat. On the eleventh day at sea, Shackleton thought he saw a clearing in the storm that had engulfed them. He realized with horror that what he saw was instead the white crest of a giant wave. It was the biggest wave he had ever seen in his 26 years on the sea.

Miraculously, the *James Caird* survived and continued to cover more than 60 miles (97 km) per day.[9] The crew was able to land the boat on South Georgia island on

May 10, 1916, after several days of being battered by storms with the island in sight. Among the most amazing accomplishments of the journey was the navigational skill of crew member Frank Worsley. The sky was clear enough for him to get their bearings just four times in more than two weeks. The rest of the time, the crew had no choice but to attempt to stay on the very same heading and hope and pray they would not miss the island and venture out into the Atlantic.

FINAL LEG

Shackleton had achieved the unbelievable in leading his freezing and frostbitten team through some of the world's most turbulent waters. Yet the whaling station on South Georgia, where the island's only people lived, lay on the other side of the island. The journey was 22 miles (35 km) over a landscape so

CAPE HORN ROLLERS

Shackleton's lifeboats were little more than rowboats equipped with sails. They were especially unsuited for the conditions just north of Antarctica, where vast stretches of open water allow for large, powerful waves. These waves are called Cape Horn rollers, named after the southernmost point of South America. They can reach heights of more than 50 feet (15 m). Some sailors have reported waves of more than 200 feet (60 m), and while these have not been officially recorded, computer models indicate waves of up to 219 feet (67 m) are possible in severe storms.[11]

EXPEDITION MAP

Shackleton ended up going in a large loop, traveling by ship, then on foot, and finally by lifeboat.

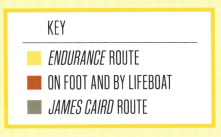

KEY

— *ENDURANCE* ROUTE
— ON FOOT AND BY LIFEBOAT
— *JAMES CAIRD* ROUTE

A LEADER FOR THE MOMENT

Surviving extreme environments involves more than securing food, water, and shelter. Avoiding panic and maintaining a positive attitude both are critical. The Shackleton expedition sheds light on the important role leadership can play in survival. Shackleton made a point of bringing his team together regularly to celebrate their successes, both big and small. In dangerous situations, Shackleton went first. He also made it a point to learn about each team member's background and interests and talk with them about the things he knew they enjoyed the most.

unknown it was blank on their map. With two of the *James Caird* crew too weak to travel, Shackleton chose two other men and set off for the whaling station on May 19. For 36 hours, the three climbed and slid down ice-covered peaks, waded through a waist-deep, icy cold river, and even used ropes to descend through a 30-foot (9 m) waterfall.[12]

Shackleton and his men arrived at the whaling station the afternoon of May 20, 1916. The station manager, with whom Shackleton had struck up a friendship before departing on the expedition in 1914, did not recognize him at first. The station manager quickly sent a ship to rescue the remaining crew of the *James Caird* on the other side of the island. Then, on May 23, Shackleton and his two crew members boarded the whaler *Southern Sky*, which they hoped to use to rescue the 22 men remaining on

▲ Photographer Frank Hurley captured a photo of the men on Elephant Island waving as Shackleton came to rescue them.

Elephant Island. Just 100 miles (160 km) from the island, the *Southern Sky* was stopped by ice.[13]

For the next three months, Shackleton mounted three more rescue attempts. Two were forced to turn back by ice. The third reached Elephant Island on August 30, 1916. It had been more than 22 months since they had left South Georgia island. All 22 expedition members were still alive.[14]

The crew of the supply ship for the original expedition plan, the *Aurora*, was not so lucky. Unlike *Endurance*, the *Aurora* had succeeded in its mission to land at Antarctica and place supplies for the travelers to use on the second half of their cross-Antarctic trek. Yet ice pulled the *Aurora* off its mooring in May 1915 while ten members of the crew were on land. The ship was unable to return to land to rescue them, and they were stranded there until Shackleton returned for them in January 1917. By that time, three of the ten had died.[15]

CHAPTER 8

SURVIVING EXTREME COLD

Modern travelers and outdoor adventurers have many tools and a lot of knowledge that were unavailable to past polar explorers. While most people will never find themselves stranded in a frigid wilderness, everyone still can benefit from learning how to manage cold temperatures. Surviving in extreme cold is a matter of being prepared, being smart, and in the event of unanticipated challenges, being ready for rescue.

The first step involves learning to pay attention to the environment and being aware of potential problems before they occur. There are many weather

◀ Backpacks can be important for holding emergency supplies in case a cold-climate adventurer gets stranded or injured.

> **I don't see bushes or trees anymore; I see tools, food and shelter.**[1]
>
> —Tyler White, creator of online survival website TJack Survival

apps for mobile phones that will provide alerts in advance of weather emergencies, such as winter storms and blizzards. When evaluating these alerts, people should pay attention to predicted windchills as well as temperatures, winds, and precipitation. Traveling and outdoor activities during these cold weather emergencies should be avoided if possible. Knowing the weather conditions several days out is important, as is regularly checking for updates in case conditions change.

If driving, the vehicle should be prepared for the journey. The vehicle's heater and defroster should be checked to see if they are working. The car should have at least half of a tank of gas or, if it is an electric car, a fully charged battery, before setting out. People should bring a cold-weather emergency kit, including a flashlight with batteries, a shovel, jumper cables, a lighter or matches, energy-dense snacks such as protein bars, a bottle or two of water, mittens, hats, socks, and a blanket. It also is a good idea to pack a red bandana or other highly visible cloth that can be waved to flag down help if needed or to mark a car that might be partially or fully buried in snow.

It also is important to dress for the weather conditions, even if the plan is to be inside a warm car the entire time. Dressing for cold requires using layers of loose-fitting, lightweight, warm clothing, with each layer performing a different function. A person does not need to be wearing all the layers when starting out, but they should be packed in the vehicle. The ideal layering pattern begins with a moisture-wicking fabric next to the skin to keep the body dry, even if a person sweats. Lightweight wool or silk fabrics are especially good for this. People should avoid cotton or other fabrics that trap moisture and take a long time to dry.

The next layer or two are for insulation. These layers should be designed to trap body heat, so they should be light and not too tight. Ideal insulating layers include

PREPARING FOR RESCUE

Among the most important elements of extreme cold survival is preparing for a potential rescue ahead of time. People should share plans, travel routes, and destinations with friends and family and agree on check-in times and a plan of action if a check-in is missed. People should bring items that allow them to be easily located. Whistles, headlamps, and brightly colored clothing can all help rescuers spot a person. Using the available resources, people should also spell out the universal distress signal, SOS. Staying near the route shared in advance with friends and family will help shorten the time it takes rescuers to find a missing person.

fleece, down, or wool. It is important to maintain heat in the body's core, so a down vest can be a good example of this layer. The final layer should protect the body from the elements, including wind and precipitation. It is sometimes necessary to unzip the outermost layers when active to avoid trapping moisture inside.

The head and neck also lose heat and need protection from the cold. Warm hats and scarves are critical to preventing heat loss because the blood vessels in these areas do not constrict in the cold like they do in the hands and feet. To avoid constricted blood vessels in hands and feet, mittens keep hands warmer than gloves. Mittens that are snug at the wrist and made of waterproof materials are ideal. Footwear also should be waterproof but flexible to allow the feet to move. It can be useful to layer socks and mittens with a thin

EVERYONE'S A SURVIVOR

Expert survival tips are as close as a phone or computer thanks to video sharing platforms. The popularity of these videos has led to a new category of bushcraft survival content creators. Among the stars in the category is Canadian Greg Ovens, who previously competed on the survival television show *Alone*. The Ovens Rocky Mountain Bushcraft channel on YouTube offers an engaging look at surviving in the Canadian Rockies. He and fellow *Alone* contestant Zachary Fowler have even teamed up on feature-length films, including one that follows their own 30-day survival challenge.

⚠ A balaclava is one type of face covering that can protect the face from cold wind and can warm the air a person breathes in.

moisture-wicking layer and a thermal layer over that. Being aware of the potential for frostbite on exposed skin can help prevent injury. A large, warm scarf can do double duty by keeping the neck, cheeks, chin, and nose covered while also reducing the amount of cold air taken into the lungs.

STAYING HEALTHY AND HYDRATED

Cold-weather activities can be fun, but they require preparation to make sure people remain safe. Regardless of activity level, it is important that people stay hydrated in cold conditions. Snow may be readily available, but eating snow can reduce the body's core temperature. It is better to melt snow over a fire or even in a canteen held next to

▲ In addition to wearing boots with good traction, people who expect to be traveling on ice can add ice cleats to their boots. These metal spikes can puncture the ice for better grip.

the body. Survival experts recommend adding more snow to a canteen after drinking to give it a head start on melting.

In addition to remaining hydrated, extreme cold survival requires careful attention to remaining injury-free. Frostbite can happen in just minutes in very cold conditions. It may be necessary to undertake survival tasks in small bursts and warm up in between. Maintaining awareness of the surroundings and working carefully to avoid making mistakes that might result in injury are important when medical care is inaccessible.

People should be on the lookout for thin ice and unstable surfaces. If possible, people should wear footwear designed to provide good traction on ice and snow when going outside or traveling in cold climates. Overexertion can leave people sweaty and at greater risk of hypothermia and injury, so taking frequent breaks to reduce sweating is helpful. Feeling sleepy or confused can be a sign of hypothermia, and anyone experiencing this symptom should try to warm up.

Someone stranded with a vehicle should stay with the vehicle, which can be found more easily than a lost person. If stranded without a vehicle, it may be necessary to construct a shelter. Snow makes an excellent insulator if it is available. Snow can be piled up or dug into, creating shelter from the wind. Snow should be packed down before being slept on, and the layers upon which a person sleeps are more important for warmth than what is on top. Once a solid sleeping base has been created, blankets and sleeping bags can add warmth both below and above the person.

It can also help to build a fire to add warmth. Making fires in snowy conditions is challenging. A spot that is out of the wind and on either bare ground or densely packed snow will provide the best chance of starting a fire. People can create a platform of dry wood and tinder. Bark shavings from trees can be dry enough to start a fire. When planning an outdoor adventure in the cold, having a fire-starting kit can be useful. Fires can also serve as signals to attract rescuers. To avoid looking like an ordinary campfire, a series of three fires set in a triangle can call attention to the situation.

PREPARE TO HAVE FUN

Extreme cold survival stories offer hope that humans can triumph over even the most challenging odds. Planning ahead can significantly help improve those odds should something go wrong. Experienced backpackers, mushers, climbers, and backcountry sports enthusiasts routinely pack

CULTURAL IMPACT
COLD SURVIVAL IN ENTERTAINMENT

Polar expeditions and wilderness survival stories have captured people's imaginations for years. Many extreme survival stories have made it to the big screen. The 2015 film *The Revenant* is based on the true story of frontiersman Hugh Glass, who was left for dead on the US frontier after being mauled by a bear in the early 1800s. Similarly, the 2019 movie *Togo* re-creates the treacherous real-life trip of musher Leonhard Seppala and his sled dogs as they raced to deliver life-saving medicine to the people of Nome, Alaska.

Video game developers have also embraced the challenges of extreme cold survival with a host of winter-based survival titles. These games require players to effectively manage limited resources, cold, and mental health challenges in a variety of settings. *Near Death* challenges players to survive after a plane crash in Antarctica. *The Long Dark* takes place in an imaginary future where players must manage their food intake, energy levels, and overall health as they navigate a frozen, danger-filled wilderness.

▼ Leonhard Seppala and Togo helped save thousands of lives when they traveled more than 260 miles (420 km) in treacherous conditions.

emergency supplies before heading out into extreme cold conditions. Outdoor adventurers seeking extra confidence in wilderness and extreme cold situations might also find it useful to take a class on survival skills and practice those skills in non-critical situations.

Prepared or not, however, the ultimate survival skill is within the brain. Humans evolved to produce an immediate physiological reaction to stressful situations to help them stay alive. This reaction results in a faster heart rate, increased blood pressure, and faster breathing rate. Psychologists call this the fight-or-flight response. Survival in extreme cold situations may require an opposite reaction of being calm, allowing a person to assess the situation, prepare a plan, and gradually implement the plan. To help reach this state of calm, experts suggest taking a series of deep breaths.

JUST STOP

Survival experts caution that the biggest threat to health and safety when lost or stranded is panic. While panic can be a normal reaction, it prevents the brain from doing what it does best, which is figuring out how to survive. To stop panic from derailing thinking, experts suggest using the STOP method: sit, think, observe, and plan. Sit down for about 30 minutes and drink some water.[2] Think about what you are facing and ask what the threats are. Observe the surrounding area and what options you notice. Finally, plan what you are going to do next.

▲ There are many ways to enjoy cold environments. Warm clothing and having a plan for emergencies can help an adventure run smoothly.

This tricks the body into believing it is in a state of relaxation, lowering its stress response and enabling more clear thinking.

Understanding how extreme cold affects the body and how it can be managed adds a new level of confidence for anyone whose plans or circumstances land them in such situations. Being prepared to meet the challenges of nature can make any winter adventure that much more enjoyable.

ESSENTIAL FACTS

SURVIVAL STORIES

- Homesteader Tyson Steele survived three weeks in the Alaskan wilderness in the heart of winter from 2019 to 2020 with little more than a wood stove and a tent. Steele focused on avoiding injury and maintaining a positive attitude.

- The 25-person Greely Expedition began as a scientific mission in 1881 to study polar weather from a camp in Nunavut, Canada. A series of storms and unfavorable ice conditions prevented a resupply of food and other provisions, leaving the party to fend for itself. Only six people survived following a rescue in 1884.

- Ada Delutuk Blackjack survived two years on the uninhabited Wrangel Island near Siberia. She went to the island in 1921 as part of a five-member team sent to claim the island for Canada. Blackjack taught herself how to trap, hunt, and build boats to survive. She was the only survivor.

- In 1963, airplane passenger Helen Klaben and pilot Ralph Flores crashed in a storm and were stranded in Canada's Yukon wilderness for nearly 50 days. The two survived by melting snow for water and using what few resources they could repurpose from their crashed plane. A bush pilot found them.

- Irish explorer Ernest Shackleton set out in the *Endurance* with a 28-member expedition in 1914 to cross Antarctica via dogsled. Pack ice eventually sunk the vessel. The expedition spent the next three years trying to make its way back to civilization, overcoming incredible odds. All crew members survived.

EXTREME COLD SURVIVAL

- Polar and tundra landscapes are among the most challenging for humans to survive because of little vegetation, limited wildlife, extended periods of darkness, extremely cold temperatures and windchills, and deadly storms.

- The harshness of cold environments also means fewer people have settled in these areas, creating vast distances between places where a lost or stranded person might find shelter, food, and medical help.

- Surviving in such landscapes requires planning ahead to secure sufficient food, warm clothing, sources of heat and shelter, and emergency supplies. In these sparsely populated areas, help may not be available should an emergency arise.

- In the absence of such planning, survivors must remain calm, assess what resources are available to them, and use those resources as efficiently as possible. Preventing further injury from frostbite and hypothermia also is critical to survival when medical care is not readily available.

QUOTE

"You can't fight [the cold]. You either adjust and dress accordingly or you suffer."

—*Resident of Yakutsk, Russia, where temperatures routinely drop below −40 degrees Fahrenheit (−40°C)*

GLOSSARY

backcountry
An area with very few roads and settlements.

bush
An area of wild land that has not been cleared or settled.

cache
A store of something, such as food, that has been hidden to protect it.

curfew
A regulation that requires people to leave the streets at a certain time.

diphtheria
A disease that affects the throat, making it hard to breathe.

frostbite
Damage to bodily tissue—particularly in the fingers, toes, and nose—due to exposure to extreme cold.

homesteader
In modern terms, a person who adopts a lifestyle focused on self-sufficiency and minimum help from other people.

ice floe
An individual piece of pack ice (sea ice) that is 66 feet (20 m) or more in diameter.

keel
Part of the central structure of a ship. The floor and frames attach to the keel.

latitude
A distance north or south of the equator, measured in degrees.

musher
A person who drives the team of dogs pulling a sled.

pack ice
A general term for sea ice.

polar
Something that is related to either the North or South Pole.

ration
A set amount of food, typically divided among members of a group so that there is enough to go around.

tundra
The biome surrounding the North Pole; the coldest biome on Earth, characterized by permafrost and lack of trees.

ADDITIONAL RESOURCES

SELECTED BIBLIOGRAPHY

Caravantes, Peggy. *Marooned in the Arctic: The True Story of Ada Blackjack, the "Female Robinson Crusoe."* Chicago Review, 2016.

"How to Avoid Needing a Winter Rescue in the Backcountry." *Appalachian Mountain Club*, 3 Feb. 2021, outdoors.org. Accessed 9 May 2023.

Todd, A. L. *Abandoned: The Story of the Greely Arctic Expedition, 1881–1884*. Papamoa, 2017.

FURTHER READINGS

Hand, Carol. *Climate Scientists*. Abdo, 2020.

Ittusardjuat, Serapio. *How I Survived: Four Nights on the Ice*. Inhabit Media, 2020.

Sonneborn, Liz. *Rock and Mountain Survival Stories*. Abdo, 2024.

ONLINE RESOURCES

To learn more about extreme cold and survival, please visit **abdobooklinks.com** or scan this QR code. These links are routinely monitored and updated to provide the most current information available.

MORE INFORMATION

For more information on this subject, contact or visit the following organizations:

GATES OF THE ARCTIC NATIONAL PARK AND PRESERVE
nps.gov/gaar/index.htm

Gates of the Arctic National Park and Preserve lies entirely north of the Arctic Circle in Alaska. Temperatures reach below −50 degrees Fahrenheit (−46°C) in the winter. People have lived here for thousands of years, and an Iñupiaq village called Anaktuvuk Pass is within the park's borders.

QUTTINIRPAAQ NATIONAL PARK
Ellesmere Island, NU, Canada
nunavut.info@pc.gc.ca
parks.canada.ca/pn-np/nu/quttinirpaaq

The Canadian government maintains the site of the Greely Expedition's Fort Conger within its Quttinirpaaq National Park. Fort Conger is open to visitors if they are accompanied by a staff member of the Parks Canada Agency. Quttinirpaaq is Canada's northernmost national park.

UNITED STATES ANTARCTIC PROGRAM
National Science Foundation
Office of Polar Programs
Geosciences Directorate
2415 Eisenhower Ave., Ste. W7100
Alexandria, VA 22314
websupport@usap.gov
usap.gov

The United States Antarctic Program manages scientific research, funding, and logistical aspects of the US presence in Antarctica. It also promotes conservation of Antarctica.

SOURCE NOTES

CHAPTER 1. UP IN SMOKE

1. Ken Marsh. "Survivor." *State of Alaska Department of Public Safety*, n.d., dps.alaska.gov. Accessed 26 July 2023.
2. "Man Survives 23 DAYS in SUBZERO Alaska Bush after OFF GRID Cabin Burns." *YouTube*, uploaded by Alison Morrow, 9 Feb. 2020, youtube.com.
3. Diane Vuković. "How to Build a Snow Cave for Winter Survival." *Primal Survivor*, 20 Dec. 2021, primalsurvivor.net. Accessed 26 July 2023.
4. Becky Bohrer. "Utah Man Survived 20 Days in Alaskan Wilderness after Fire Destroyed His Cabin." *Salt Lake Tribune*, 11 Jan. 2020, sltrib.com. Accessed 26 July 2023.
5. "Man Survives 23 DAYS."
6. "Man Survives 23 DAYS."
7. "Man Survives 23 DAYS."
8. Beth Oller. "What Is Hypothermia?" *Familydoctor.org*, Dec. 2022, familydoctor.org. Accessed 26 July 2023.
9. Jess Thomson. "Winter Storm Could Freeze You to Death before You Even Know It." *Newsweek*, 21 Dec. 2022, newsweek.com. Accessed 26 July 2023.
10. Thomson, "Winter Storm Could Freeze You."
11. Natasha Lavender. "This Is the Point When Cold Weather Becomes Dangerous." *Ladders*, 11 Jan. 2019, theladders.com. Accessed 26 July 2023.
12. Peter Preskar. "Anna Bågenholm—The Woman Who Cheated Death." *Medium*, 28 Nov. 2021, short-history.com. Accessed 26 July 2023.
13. Lavender, "When Cold Weather Becomes Dangerous."

CHAPTER 2. DANGERS OF EXTREME COLD

1. Charles Q. Choi. "Which Is Colder: The North or South Pole?" *Live Science*, 5 June 2022, livescience.com. Accessed 26 July 2023.
2. "Climate—Antarctica." *Climates to Travel*, n.d., climatestotravel.com. Accessed 26 July 2023.
3. "Arctic Peoples." *Arctic Council*, n.d., arctic-council.org. Accessed 26 July 2023.
4. Rachel D'Oro. "Subzero Survivors." *Ocala StarBanner*, 17 Feb. 2004, ocala.com. Accessed 26 July 2023.
5. Jenna Russell. "Brutal Cold Sweeps across New York and New England." *New York Times*, 4 Feb. 2023, nytimes.com. Accessed 26 July 2023.
6. "Northern and Southern Hemisphere: An Overview." *Toppr*, n.d., toppr.com. Accessed 26 July 2023.
7. "Monthly: Climate Bismarck—North Dakota." *US Climate Data*, n.d., usclimatedata.com. Accessed 26 July 2023.
8. "January Weather in Bern Switzerland." *Weather Spark*, n.d., weatherspark.com. Accessed 26 July 2023.
9. *Extreme Cold: A Prevention Guide to Promote Your Personal Health and Safety*. Centers for Disease Control and Prevention, n.d., cdc.gov. Accessed 26 July 2023.
10. Heather Chen. "It's Now Minus 80°F in the World's Coldest City." *CNN*, 18 Jan. 2023, cnn.com. Accessed 26 July 2023.
11. Natasha Lavender. "This Is the Point When Cold Weather Becomes Dangerous." *Ladders*, 11 Jan. 2019, theladders.com. Accessed 26 July 2023.
12. Natalie Healey. "Extreme Cold Is Bringing Humans Back from the Brink of Death." *WIRED*, 5 Feb. 2020, wired.co.uk. Accessed 26 July 2023.
13. Judson Jones and Jenna Russell. "Northeast Braces for the Worst Wind Chill in Decades." *New York Times*, 2 Feb. 2023, nytimes.com. Accessed 26 July 2023.

14. John Enger. "Frozen. Thawed. Not Dead: Jean Hilliard's Amazing Minnesota Story." *MPR News*, 25 Jan. 2018, mprnews.org. Accessed 26 July 2023.

15. "Hypothermia: Understanding and Prevention." *University of Minnesota Duluth*, 23 Mar. 2021, seagrant.umn.edu. Accessed 26 July 2023.

16. "Hypothermia."

CHAPTER 3. THREE WEEKS IN ALASKA

1. Joshua St. Clair. "If the Fire Goes Out." *Esquire*, 26 Feb. 2021, esquire.com. Accessed 26 July 2023.

2. "Man Survives 23 DAYS in SUBZERO Alaska Bush after OFF GRID Cabin Burns." *YouTube*, uploaded by Alison Morrow, 9 Feb. 2020, youtube.com.

3. "Man Survives 23 DAYS."

4. "A WWII Survival Story from the Charley River." *National Park Service*, 20 Aug. 2020, nps.gov. Accessed 26 July 2023.

5. "Man Survives 23 DAYS."

6. Ken Marsh. "Survivor." *State of Alaska Department of Public Safety*, n.d., dps.alaska.gov. Accessed 26 July 2023.

7. "Man Survives 23 DAYS."

8. "Man Survives 23 DAYS."

9. Dan Kraker. "Duluth 14-Year-Old Has Slept Outside for 1,021 Straight Nights, and Still Counting." *MPR News*, 3 Feb. 2023, mprnews.org. Accessed 26 July 2023.

CHAPTER 4. ABANDONED IN THE ARCTIC

1. "First International Polar Year (1882–83): *Encyclopedia Arctica 7: Meteorology and Oceanography*." Encyclopedia Arctica, 1947–51, collections.dartmouth.edu. Accessed 26 July 2023.

2. "The Greely Expedition: Timeline." *PBS American Experience*, n.d., pbs.org. Accessed 26 July 2023.

3. "Timeline."

4. "Timeline."

5. "Timeline."

6. "The Greely Expedition: Trailer." *PBS American Experience*, 5 Feb. 2019, pbs.org. Accessed 26 July 2023.

7. "Arctic Exploration: The Demise of the 1881 Greely Expedition." *Viewpoints Radio*, 19 Jan. 2020, viewpointsradio.org. Accessed 26 July 2023.

8. "Greely Expedition: Trailer."

9. "Timeline."

10. A. L. Todd. *Abandoned: The Story of the Greely Arctic Expedition, 1881–1884*. Papamoa, 2017. 184.

11. "How Many Calories Does a Polar Explorer Need?" *Encounter Edu*, n.d., encounteredu.com. Accessed 26 July 2023.

12. Todd, *Abandoned*, 192.

13. Todd, *Abandoned*, 212.

14. "Arctic Exploration."

SOURCE NOTES CONTINUED

CHAPTER 5. HEROINE OF WRANGEL ISLAND

1. "Serum Run of 1925." *Alaska State Archives*, 26 Sept. 2019, archives.alaska.gov. Accessed 26 July 2023.
2. Jon Wertheim. "And You Thought *We* Have Vaccine Issues?" *Sports Illustrated*, 13 Jan. 2021, si.com. Accessed 26 July 2023.
3. "Serum Run of 1925."
4. Peggy Caravantes. *Marooned in the Arctic: The True Story of Ada Blackjack, the "Female Robinson Crusoe."* Chicago Review, 2016. 2–3.
5. Caravantes, *Marooned in the Arctic*, 104.
6. Tessa Hulls. "Ada Blackjack: The Forgotten Sole Survivor of an Odd Arctic Expedition." *Atlas Obscura*, 6 Dec. 2017, atlasobscura.com. Accessed 26 July 2023.
7. "Ada Blackjack: Stranded on Wrangel Island." *National Park Service*, 31 May 2023, nps.gov. Accessed 26 July 2023.
8. Eric Regehr. "Polar Bears on Wrangel Island." *Polar Bears International*, 13 Sept. 2021, polarbearsinternational.org. Accessed 26 July 2023.
9. Peter Rowe. "Vilhjalmur Stefansson, Ada Blackjack, and the Canadian Invasion of Russia." *Canadian Geographic*, 11 Mar. 2022, canadiangeographic.ca. Accessed 26 July 2023.
10. Caravantes, *Marooned in the Arctic*, 67.
11. Caravantes, *Marooned in the Arctic*, 91, 99.
12. Kieran Mulvaney. "The Inuit Woman Who Survived Alone on an Arctic Island after a Disastrous Expedition." *History*, 17 Nov. 2021, history.com. Accessed 26 July 2023.

CHAPTER 6. MIRACLE IN THE YUKON

1. P. D. Peacock. "Hey, I'm Alive." *Wilderness Innovation*, 21 Dec. 2011, wildernessinnovation.com. Accessed 26 July 2023.
2. "Hey, I'm Alive! Part 1." *Whitehorse Star*, 27 Mar. 1963, whitehorsestar.com. Accessed 26 July 2023.
3. Jimmy Smothers. "Young Soldier's Grandfather at Center of Famous Survival Tale." *Gadsden Times*, 25 Dec. 2010, gadsentimes.com. Accessed 26 July 2023.
4. "Learn about the Yukon." *Government of Canada*, 24 July 2023, canada.ca. Accessed 26 July 2023.
5. "Legendary Crash Survivor Returns to City." *Whitehorse Star*, 15 July 1996, whitehorsestar.com. Accessed 26 July 2023.
6. Peacock, "Hey, I'm Alive."
7. Smothers, "Famous Survival Tale."
8. Chad. "A 50 Year Old Tale of Survival." *Master Woodsman*, 25 Mar. 2013, masterwoodsman.com. Accessed 26 July 2023.
9. Smothers, "Famous Survival Tale."

CHAPTER 7. AGAINST INCREDIBLE ODDS

1. Alfred Lansing. *Endurance: Shackleton's Incredible Voyage*. Carroll & Graf, 1999. 17–18.
2. Lansing, *Endurance*, 23.
3. "Shackleton *Endurance* Expedition 1914–1917 - Trans-Antarctica: 2 - Trapped and Crushed." *Cool Antarctica*, n.d., coolantarctica.com. Accessed 26 July 2023.
4. Ernest Shackleton. "OCEAN CAMP Chapter 5: South!" *Cool Antarctica*, n.d., coolantarctica.com. Accessed 26 July 2023.
5. "Shackleton's Voyage of *Endurance*: Timeline." *NOVA*, Feb. 2002, pbs.org. Accessed 26 July 2023.
6. Jody Rosen. "The Discovery of Shackleton's Wreck Is as Disquieting as It Is Amazing." *New York Times*, 30 Mar. 2022, nytimes.com. Accessed 26 July 2023.
7. "Trans-Antarctica: 2 - Trapped and Crushed."
8. Lansing, *Endurance*, 181.
9. "Trans-Antarctica: 2 - Trapped and Crushed."
10. Lansing, *Endurance*, 202.
11. Jerry Dennis and Glenn Wolf. "Waves: Freak Waves and Rogues." *Bird in the Waterfall*, 1996, leelanau.com. Accessed 26 July 2023.
12. "Shackleton *Endurance* Expedition 1914–1917 - Trans-Antarctica: 4 - Rescue." *Cool Antarctica*, n.d., coolantarctica.com. Accessed 26 July 2023.
13. "Shackleton's Voyage of *Endurance*."
14. "Trans-Antarctica: 4 - Rescue."
15. Tom Crean. "January 10, 1917: The Aurora Rescue." *Tom Crean*, 9 Jan. 2016, tomcreandiscovery.com. Accessed 26 July 2023.

CHAPTER 8. SURVIVING EXTREME COLD

1. Tyler White. "Home Page." *TJack Survival*, n.d., tjacksurvival.com. Accessed 26 July 2023.
2. Nick Clement. "Outdoor Survival Series: Controlling Panic." *Colorado Outdoors*, 9 Mar. 2016, coloradooutdoorsmag.com. Accessed 26 July 2023.

INDEX

Alaska, 5–6, 10–11, 20, 32, 35, 51–53, 63–65, 66, 97
animals, 20, 47–48, 51, 53, 55, 58, 60–61, 76–77
  dogs, 6, 44, 52, 58, 77, 97
  polar bears, 20, 55, 57, 60
Antarctic, 17–19, 22, 75, 77–78, 80, 84, 85, 87, 97
  South Pole, 18–19, 21, 75–76, 85
Arctic, 17–22, 37–39, 42, 44, 48, 51, 53, 55, 58, 66
  North Pole, 18–19, 38
Arviat, 43
Aurora, 75, 87

Bågenholm, Anna, 14
Blackjack, Ada Delutuk, 51–61
Blackjack, Bennett, 52–53, 61
brown fat, 13

Camp Clay, 43–44
Canada, 20–21, 38, 53, 55, 65, 66, 92
  British Columbia, 65, 66
  Yukon, 65, 66, 73
Cape Horn rollers, 84
Cape Sabine, 42–46, 49
clothing, 5–6, 8, 11, 25, 47, 48, 53, 56, 82, 83, 90–93
Crawford, Allan, 53, 58–59

Endurance, 76–80, 82, 85, 87

fire, 5–6, 9–12, 29–31, 34, 47, 69, 72, 93, 96
Flores, Ralph, 63–73
food, 6, 11, 25, 30, 34–35, 42–49, 51–52, 55, 57–58, 68–69, 72–73, 86, 90, 93, 97
Fort Conger, 38, 39, 40, 42–43
Fowler, Zachary, 92
frostbite, 11, 25–26, 73, 82, 84, 93–95

Galle, Milton, 53–54, 56–59
Greely, Adolphus, 37, 40, 42–44, 47–49
Greely, Henrietta, 49
Greely Expedition, 37–49

Hilliard, Jean, 26
homelessness, 20, 25
hydration, 23, 47, 93–95
hypothermia, 11, 13, 23–25, 44, 95

ice, 11, 13, 14, 17, 20, 26–27, 33, 38, 40, 42–43, 46–47, 55, 57–58, 61, 66, 77–80, 83, 85, 86–87, 95
Imperial Trans-Antarctic Expedition, 75, 79
Iñupiaq people, 51–52

James Caird, 82–83, 85, 86

Klaben, Helen, 63–73
Knight, Errol Lorne, 53–54, 56–60

Long Dark, The, 97

Maurer, Frederick, 53–54, 56–59
moisture, 15, 23, 26, 44, 91–93

navigation, 33, 77, 83–84, 97
Near Death, 97

ocean, 18–19, 79, 85
Ocean Camp, 79
Ortman, Isaac, 35
Ovens, Greg, 92
Ovens Rocky Mountain Bushcraft, 92

Paulet Island, 80
polar vortex, 21

Revenant, The, 97
Ross Sea, 75–76

search and rescue, 35, 43, 49, 61, 68–69, 72, 91
Shackleton, Ernest, 75, 77–81, 83–84, 86–87

shelter, 5–6, 10–12, 20, 29, 31–35, 43, 46–47, 56, 61, 68–70, 82, 86, 90, 95–96
Siberia, Russia, 19, 53–54, 58
snow blindness, 60, 61
snow caves, 10
SOS, 30, 31, 33, 70–72, 91
South Georgia island, 77, 79, 81, 83–84, 85, 87
Steele, Tyson, 5–13, 29–35
Stefansson, Vilhjalmur, 55, 61
STOP method, 98
storms, 22, 57–58, 65, 83–84, 90

temperatures, 5, 13–15, 18–19, 21–27, 29, 32, 35, 41, 44, 47, 52, 57–58, 65–66, 78, 89–90, 93
Togo, 97

vehicles, 26, 39–40, 42–43, 44, 46, 49, 52, 54–55, 57–58, 61, 75–80, 82–83, 84, 85, 86–87, 90–91, 95
Verkhoyansk, Russia, 19

water, 6, 15, 18–19, 26–27, 35, 43, 46–47, 61, 69, 73, 79, 83–84, 86, 90, 98
Weddell Sea, 76, 81, 85
windchill, 13–14, 21, 25, 90
Wrangel Island, 53–56

ABOUT THE AUTHOR

JILL C. WHEELER

Jill C. Wheeler is the author of more than 300 nonfiction titles for young readers. Her interests include behavioral sciences, sustainable agriculture, and any kind of travel. She lives in Minneapolis, Minnesota, where she enjoys sailing, riding motorcycles, and reading.